I would like to thank everyone for picking up this book and allowing my thoughts in to your homes.

I also would like to thank Barbara Spencer, Jennifer Martin and Latitia O'Daye for the critique and edits. More to come, so ride this journey with me. Peace and Love

Table of Contents

8 Conversations to Have With Your Co-Parent

John Martin Sr.

Other books by Author
www.rodneytheordinarykidchronicles.com
www.8conversationstohave.com

Intro

I'm back! Yes, once again I'm working on the development of the American family since this is so important to me. I write this book in hopes of touching the souls of the old, young, black, white or green. I write this in thought of my past experiences with my co-parent(s), and how my childhood played a big role in how I handled certain situations.

What we teach on a daily basis is what we have learned, and we are always teaching someone around us. The typical adult has so many habits that rub off on our surroundings, sometimes we do not consciously intend on teaching, but we must understand IT is happening whether we are paying attention or not.

I bring up my childhood a lot as an adult. I recall it was filled with endless nights of hearing screaming and yelling coming from the basement where my step dad and mother would be. After years of dealing with constant chaos, I would stand at the top of the staircase with one ear intentionally poked out towards the direction of the yelling; with one fist balled up and one fist clutching a broom, or an iron. I would clutch anything of weight that I could use to knock this guy out "if I hear him touch my mother" I would think to myself... I cannot count how many times my siblings and I had to step up to [be the adults] and mediate a petty situation between the grown- ups of the house.

Later, during my own son's upbringing, I recall me acting the same way, arguing back and forth with his mother. Early on, I couldn't imagine the trauma that may have been inflicted into my son. Being a young parent, I always gave my kids more credit than they probably deserved. I probably gave my co-parents and me more credit than we deserved as well. I recall times of me yelling and seeing my son across the room thinking in my head, "oh he doesn't know what's going on," or, "I didn't say these foul words loud enough for him to hear. He's ok!" However, in the heat of an irrational moment, I had no clue of the picture I was painting through his eyes. It didn't matter to me so much until recently, when I started thinking about what messages I would like to leave behind. I started thinking how can I make my family better and how can I right my wrongs? In my quest to right my wrongs, I thought about my interactions with my kids. I have sat down and talked about their views and how they see me as a parent. I look back over the years and realize all of the mistakes I have made by putting them in broken homes. I want to change this. I want to teach the world that the most powerful structure is the family. It took me years to realize the destruction I've caused, and the inability to decipher right and wrong harmed my way of thinking. Hopefully, I can help some parents out there change sooner than I did. It takes some of us awhile, because we must unlearn and relearn, but it's worth the process. The empowerment formed from a well-oiled machine working with all the parts joining, provides fruit. The cycle of our children learning the bad and outweighing the great has to be stopped. It is up to us to change our mindsets and adapt to raising our children strong, so twenty years from now we are living in a better world. 20 years? Think back 20 years ago. It was just yesterday, like really! When you grasp the concept of truly knowing time is flying, you understand what you do today indeed DOES affect tomorrow. I open up this book for everyone in mind, however I want to really target the young parent. I want this for the young men and women that have a child, which is a precious mind they are molding. I want this for the parent that wants to do well for their child, but lacks the effective communication skills to work productively with their co-parent. I want to touch the parent that needs guidance and direction on how to pull themselves up from the trauma they saw in their past. I want to reach the parent that needs to get through to the other parent. I want to touch the parent that has a dream of creating a strong family. We all have to build. What is your process of building? Don't worry, I'll wait.

Chapter 1
The Family Structure: Foundation

Did you know in recent years, I did a research paper on traits of people that are incarcerated? I don't recall the exact percent (forgot the source, but you can google this info also), but I think it was 85% of people in prison come from fatherless homes. Alarming? Indeed. 60 % of suicides were people that grew up with no father. I bring this up early just to set the tone of what I am saying next. The family structure is important! It is the blueprint for potential wealth building, the domain for emotional support, and a team-driven navigational system. When I think of the family structure in a specific way, I think of two parents and then, kids. The two parents are the psychologists, the motivators, the leaders, the teachers, groomers and providers. That leaves the children to be the students who are dependent for so many things, but most parents are motivated by their children. This structure is a circle where each individual participant feeds off of each other. You might think that your child needs you, and you are very well correct. They will need you for a certain time frame of their lives. However, most parents that get to interact with their child and have a solid connection, realize that *they* need their child. Children motivate parents! Children drive parents to become more than what they would have ever imagined when they were younger. How many times have you heard a parent say, "If it wasn't for my kids..."? I have said it plenty of times. Me personally, if it wasn't for my kids, I wouldn't be living. I'm sure I would be dead or in jail. So, the importance of the family structure is vital for every component. The foundation that the balance of having a mother and a father provides the child is crucial. It is important for a child to be able to see and feel balance from having a mother and a father.

I understand relationships don't work out. I also understand some 'baby daddy/baby momma' situations happen from a one-night stand. So, the traditional family structured household isn't always possible, but we need to define another way. The 'baby mama' or 'baby daddy' terminology lessens and devalues the powerful role we fulfill as parents. Think of how many times you have heard, "Oh, that's just my baby daddy". That saying subconsciously devalues the role of a father. People call their co-parents "baby mama" and "baby daddy" even when the child is well beyond being a baby. If we defined the role with a higher status or title, it would subconsciously change how we understand how serious our role is. Instead of saying baby mama or baby daddy, how about "he is my son's father" or, "she is my daughter's mother." It sounds so simple, but the words we use shape our thoughts and our actions so we must mean what we say and say what we mean. We must intentionally put our family structure higher. The role of being a co-parent starts no later than when the baby is born and well into adulthood. At the minimum, you are looking at 18 years of communicating with your co-parent. 18 years of sharing disciplinary roles and other parenting moments that can be very challenging. You can make the best out of these times, or you can make the times hard for one another. If I were to talk to my kids' mother back then after what I know now after 20 years, the conversation would go a little bit like this:

"Wow, we are bringing a human being into this world! This is so real. We have the ability to shape and mold a future leader. We have the ability to shape and mold our thoughts into this little one. I am the father of your child. I am not your baby daddy. I will do my part and then some to make sure my son/daughter understands his/herself and the world around him/her. We will do a lot of growing, all 3 of us, and growing takes learning and unlearning. We must communicate, which means listen to one another. Listen to our child. We should come together and make the best decisions for him/her. Our family structure is set. You are my child's mother & I am your child's father. Whatever or whomever comes along, they will have to respect what we have because our foundation is set around us raising our child. We must talk about so many things, and I'm sure we will get on each other's nerves at times, but we must come back to the foundation, which is our child. We must live righteous and be able to support one another.

If we don't do that, our child will suffer. We are supposed to be grown, we are going to make it one way or another. If we don't make it, that is on us, but providing opportunities for our child is our responsibility, and we must cherish our task. We protect our obligations. We don't have to like each other but we have to respect our role in this. We created our future together. Yes, we laid down and created our future TOGETHER. If you go marry, I'm still going to be here. If I go marry someone, you will still be here. Let's make teamwork happen. The strongest asset a child has is his/her family. The biggest asset parents have is their child."

Chapter 2

Postpartum Depression and other life-altering situations

A woman's body goes through so many changes during pregnancy. I mean, think about it. A human being is growing inside of her. The little human is feeding off of her and using her nutrients. Psychologically, she is changing also. They say a woman is never the same after they have a child. In the first of the three trimesters, the mother can feel fatigue, mood swings, appetite changes, anxiety and depression. She will go on emotional roller coasters and maybe say a lot of things she doesn't mean. This continues and increases throughout the whole 9 months of pregnancy. However, fellas, what you might not be aware of are the affects and changes that continue AFTER the pregnancy. She might not want to be touched. Her hormones are all over the place. She might feel low. Depression attacks women during and after pregnancy. Rationality is affected, and making the best decisions can be challenging. THIS is where we men must be more understanding. This is where we must learn to communicate better because of this life changing experience. Postpartum depression is real, and if it isn't treated correctly, it can last for a long time. Men can also have postpartum depression. Be aware! How many of us have been in great relationships up until the point of being parents with each other? A lot of us know how to have a good time, cherish our partner until it's time to be a parent and then, BOOM! We change! Well, we do! We change big time. We have added self-doubt, uncertainty and stress into the equation. However, we must learn as we go that we need to work better in these situations. We men go through so much during the first few stages of parenting as well. We are hit with the stresses of being providers for the little one. We are hit with being uncertain about the future. We deal with our sexual needs not being met at times, because our woman is not feeling the same. She is going through her moments of depression and other stresses. Her body has changed and she isn't feeling as attractive. She isn't feeling as sexual as once before. We fellas struggle with this sometimes because we don't do the research. We don't understand it isn't us that she isn't attracted to anymore. It is the situation that needs to be pampered and comforted. We must do more research about how things are changing and be mature enough to grasp, comprehend and handle. We must handle our duties to make our situations better. That may mean read books on how to handle your partner's stress. Think of ways to be more comforting, and compromise at times. We are dealing with the stresses of our thoughts changing, as well as our lifestyles. We just went from coming and going as we please, not having a care in the world, to now adapting to being responsible for another human every second of the day. This is a huge transition that we need to talk about more between the co-parents. This journey is challenging for both, and we each have so many issues that need to be recognized early. We must understand each other's position.

If you are not with your co-parent, that is fine. The way the world is set up, we understand things happen. However, we obviously need to still be present in our child's life. The better the relationship is between you and your co-parent, the better chance you have of setting your child up for the win. We can break bad cycles by educating ourselves on the female anatomy, and mental health after pregnancy. There are support groups out here for new fathers. We can also mention google again and again. There is no excuse for either parent to be naive about each other's feelings and mental health. We must take time to learn each other.

Not getting educated on how to deal with and recognize your co-parent's changes is setting yourself up for disaster. Arguments will surely follow. Here comes the trying to get your point across and she/he isn't listening because they are yelling back. Here comes the abandonment. Here comes the walk outs and the door slams. Here come the long sits in the car trying to figure it all out on YOUR OWN. Here come the countless sleepless nights trying to figure it out on YOUR OWN. Is it being selfish? Do you really need to be understood before you grasp the understanding of what needs to be done in THIS situation that concerns your child? It's not about you, right? It's about making sure you know how to deal with yourself so you can deal with your baby, yourself AND your co-parent. Your co-parent might have PTSD, or battle depression. They may have addiction issues that you need to be aware of. Addictions can sprout from stress. These issues can affect the well- being of your child. If I could go back in time, this is a conversation I would have had with my co-parents:

"We both are new to this. Having a child is life-changing. On top of all of our differences we have from our upbringing, we now come together and go half on the biggest responsibility of our lives. We must deal with the changes physically and mentally, and even if we don't stay together forever, let's make a commitment to be there for one another to see our child through to adulthood. It is scary for me like this is for you. Do you understand the changes your body is about to make? They say your memory will not be the same after childbirth. I understand this. I need to read up on all of these changes your body will be making so we can help educate each other. You aren't alone in this. We will make it happen. Understand, as a man and a provider I'm going to be frustrated. We go through the postpartum also. Just like we gain weight right along with you during the pregnancy, we feel your pains on top of our own. I like to handle things on my own though, but I won't now because we have to build together. So, I will be talking more about how I feel and questions I have. We both have to talk more and listen more. The more we talk, the less 'scatterbrained' we both will be. We need a tremendous amount of focus and postpartum depression causes lack of concentration. So, when you get frustrated because your thoughts are all over the place, relax and breathe, and I can help you through; and vice- versa. We will need each other for these emotional things. The tighter we are, the tighter our plans can be, and our child will benefit from this big time."

Chapter 3
Your child

Let me take a moment to explain what meeting my dad after 33 years of life did for me...let me take you back first. As a child, I struggled with identity issues! I had a step dad for a while, but he didn't look like me. I couldn't relate. My confidence was low. I had to figure out a lot of things on my own. I did a lot of self-talking. I tried to escape reality by smoking weed and drinking. I got caught up in the false-confidence materialistic things gave me for the moment. I sold drugs because I was addicted to spending money on materials to make me "look better." I got older and ruined relationships with certain women that were down for me. I destroyed a lot by not knowing the power I had was being used in poor ways. There is a saying, 'people know right from wrong'...well, this isn't always true and being a boy growing up to be a man, you must be taught certain things to understand. Sometimes, it doesn't just come. So now...fast forward to my first ever interaction with my pops. I was 33 years old. I will never forget; I was in Miami visiting my baby sister at her graduation. I walk in the house and there goes my dad.... sitting there looking like he just walked out of a photo shoot. Super clean! The few strands of hair on his head were perfectly laid. He didn't say much. He stood up and we hugged. He sat back down and started mingling with everyone in the room. I could tell he was very articulate; he stuttered a lot though. I caught myself just staring at him. I finally saw where my hands came from. I saw where my light complexion and freckles came from. I saw how he walked, how he talked. Wow! He was me! Like I said, he didn't talk much. He didn't have to. I understood everything from that point forward. When it was time to leave, I turned to the door and walked through the doorway a brand-new man! My chin was up in the air. You couldn't tell me anything about me. I understood who I was from that point forward. The amount of confidence I received from that one hour and maybe 100 words spoken from my pops, absolutely changed my life forever. I no longer have any curiosity of who I am, because I now know! I seen it! I felt so alive! I felt like no one can stop me! I still feel unstoppable to this day, because I finally have closure. I seen where I come from. At 33, my interpretations of what I seen would obviously be different than if I was seeing this from a young age. At a young age, you would absorb your parents' actions and characteristics naturally. It would be second nature from a few times of repetition. At 33, I had to seek it on my own and pay attention. I had to play 'catch up' from all the years of absence.

Just imagine the confidence I would have had if my biological dad was a part of my life growing up. Like me seeing him! Seeing?? Let me tell you something. I knew early on in my child's life that I had to walk the walk, and walk a certain way, and carry myself in a civilized manner. As I would drive & my son would be in his car seat in the back seat, every time I looked in the rearview mirror, he would be staring at me. Now, follow me, this all ties in. I would constantly look in my rearview and there goes his eyes penetrating me with no expression on his face. When I would be in the bathroom brushing my teeth, this little guy would be staring at me. He would be learning me. When he got old enough to walk, he would walk behind me and years later, he grew accustomed to walking like me. This is what parents do! We as parents, do so much more than just buy toys, food, lecture, and discipline. We provide self-esteem by providing a blueprint of ourselves... without even being intentional!! Read that again if you need to. We provide identity! Both of us do, the mother and the father! It is so important for our kids to see where they 'get it' from. You are empowering your child by working with the mother. You are empowering your child by working with the father. You are empowering your child by BEING the father. You are empowering your child by BEING the mother. You are empowering your child by working together. This is huge! The more you understand this role, the less you will create obstacles for your co-parent to interact with your child. Now yes, you might say "Well, what if the co-parent is not stable enough to be around my child?" or "What if the co-parent is on drugs?" I say provide a structured visit. Your child is strong. They will see and learn what not to do also. I learned so much from my step dad of what not to do from his drug abuse. I used to watch him after he used drugs and I'd say "Never will that be me". I am proud to say I have never gone down that road. Even seeing so many of my people dibble and dabble in certain drugs, I stayed away from all of that. I went through that life as a young kid watching my step dad destroy himself and everything around him, so I learned my lesson. Your child may need to see the harsh realities of the co-parent's addictions. What educates us better than real life? Now, it's not what you do, it's how you do it. You can explain to your child in a way they can grasp. This takes educating yourself on how to communicate certain lessons to your child. Learning at a young age about some of your parent's faults can be powerful and very good for you. We are all learning life every day, so sometimes blocking experiences can be harmful.

Anyway, back to your child. Your child needs you and your co-parent. They need balance. They need to see your good and see your bad.

They need to see a healthy partnership between you and your co-parent. There is too much drama and negativity that we are forced to see going on in this world through media outlets, internet, music, etc. If they can see mama treating daddy right and vice versa, that is a valuable step towards cohesiveness. Even if we aren't in the same household, we can still be tight with a unique bond.

Your child may not express this, but they want you and your co-parent to be together. It doesn't matter how good the step parent is, they still have a picture of mom and dad in their mind. That isn't necessarily a bad thing, especially when both of you are showing your child the best relationship possible. When both of you are motivated to show your son/daughter the best life, everyone around the both of you will glow and be happy, not just your child. In order to give your child the best life possible, you have to provide the best YOU possible. Doing so eliminates the hate from your heart and the combative you.

Children are our greatest investment. As I said earlier, when most of us reading this can say "If it wasn't for my kids, I wouldn't care about...." or, " If it wasn't for my kids, I would be in trouble..." This is reality. Our kids are what drives many of us to keep going. If you see your co-parent going through some things, maybe creating healthy situations of interaction would help them get out of their slump.

Your child is also brutally honest. Children have a way of letting you know if you need to step it up a notch. Investing in your child is never a waste of time. Sometimes the most valuable and biggest lessons to teach your son/daughter seem so small to us. Why is that? Because the biggest lessons we hold on to, we have heard a million times. After hearing them so many times, the lessons are instilled in us and they seem common knowledge. Well, everything we know, we had to learn- same thing with your child. Old news to us is new to them. They need to hear what we heard millions of times as well.

You keep arguing back and forth in front of your child, guess what? They are learning how to be verbally abusive. You and your co-parent are working together to plan a birthday party for your child. Guess what? Your child is learning how to plan and work with others. Your child's brain is literally a sponge for everything. They are very intuitive, and their eyes are wide open to the world. They want you to teach them everything.

"Our child is a perfect blend of you and I. Isn't it absolutely intriguing that we created a human being that has both of our ways running through them? Every time I look at our child, I see you and I know you see me. Our child acts like both of us. The more and more I see our child engage and live life, I start to understand YOU more. Looking at our child gives me an idea of who you were and are to this day. Why? Because our child is YOU! If we pay more attention to our child, we will learn our ways as well. We must learn each other's language because we must communicate to conquer our task. Let's not be enemies. We are joined together by our child."

John Martin Sr.

Chapter 4
The Power of a Power Couple

Now, of course it's too late for a lot of us to have the greatest relationship with our co-parents. Some of them have crossed the line and can't come back from that. Understood! However, the young couple that just had a baby can definitely boss up from this chapter. The cliché term 'two is better than one' is real. Life is just easier with two people working together and having each other's best interest. I'm not saying relationships are always the greatest, but you have a strong chance of being less stressed if you are with the right person in the right situation. If I could go back, I would have tried to build an empire with my co-parents. It only makes sense after seeing my kids being older. They would have been set up with so much more. If you are able to communicate with each other, do so. Two parents coming together and building a life for their child is the most powerful thing you can do. Just think, what else can you build from day one, every day besides a business? Your child. If you can take a minimum of 20 minutes a day talking to your co-parent about your child, that investment alone gives your child an incredible edge. It also gives you a sense of direction and it keeps both parents motivated. Look, you aren't always going to get along, but the task is bigger than you. Why not build and make the best out of the cards you've been dealt? You might hate the individual you laid down with, but you created life with that person. Redirect your aim and get over your hatred. Develop a useful relationship! Out of 8 billion people on the earth, why be enemies with the one you created life with? I'm not saying fall in love. I'm not even saying be together. All I'm saying is keep the most important task, just that...the most important task.

Just think, if you had a routine of calling your co-parent once a day and went over your child's behavior, shared financial responsibilities, and maybe even a motivational pep talk (who knows, maybe one of you are feeling down and needs some encouragement to keep fighting and building), that would be generating an incredible amount of power. The power of building a foundation of wealth, and a high emotional IQ is essential. Look at how you are giving your son/daughter balance, and the "best of both worlds". I often say the power of two people building life together is insanely dangerous. Dangerous for the oppressors that like to keep us stagnate and down. The human family structure is the missing piece of the puzzle. Back in the 60's and mid 70's, our communities were building empires. How was this happening? It happened because we had families. When crack cocaine was introduced to our neighborhoods, it killed a lot of our families. Removing the male out of the family was a huge part of the mass destruction process of keeping us down. Women can get government assistance, as long as that man is not in the house. Nowadays, it is trendy to not "need a man"... more on that in later publications. But for now, we are talking about the power of a power couple and we must get back to this.

You might ask, "What if we have moved on and we are in a different relationship?" That's a great question with an easy answer. The answer is to take that partner with you! Sounds easy, but it takes real consistent work to make this happen. Some people are jealous. You might have a partner that does not like you having a good relationship with someone from the opposite sex, especially someone you created a baby with. Well, guess what? They are just going to have to be accepting because your child is the priority. Your child needs you and you must take care of your obligations in order to be the best you. Let's talk about this, because getting your mate to be accepting of this is sometimes a headache. But it's not WHAT you do, it's HOW you do it. First, you may have to break the insecurities in your partner. Explain to them your task is to build the best life possible for your child and you would like them to be a part of that. Explain that this task requires everyone involved to work together. So, your mate needs to establish a relationship with your child and your co-parent. The more you all are in tune with an action plan, the better. Involve your mate and establish responsibilities with them and your co-parent. If your partner isn't able to do this, then they might not be right for you. You can't go through life creating lives and not giving adequate effort to creating the best life for what you create. You also want to look at your choice of a mate. If you choose someone that isn't healthy for your lifestyle, then you need to re-evaluate your choice. Nothing is better than a family unit. Power couples have the ability to provide emotional support, security, financial gains, resources, great examples, etc.

If you aren't willing to work on collaborating and working as a whole to make things work for your child, you may be too selfish. You might need to have a real look in the mirror and see why you aren't putting more towards your child.

"Look, we need to make this work for our child. We need to teach our child to be civilized. We have to unite this power that we each possess and learn how to use it together. Yeah, it is going to take time, but we need diligent effort. We need to make it happen. If I hear of a way you can make money, or put you in a better position, I will let you know and you do the same for me. You benefiting me and me benefitting you only helps as a whole. It definitely helps our child. Us parents working against each other is so silly & immature. The uprising of power couples is the new wave.

Even if we aren't together, we can work together to produce the best product possible. Knowing that you are doing what is best for our child, and you have our child's best interest in mind makes it easier for me to accept you and grow with you. Our child will benefit immensely. Just think if we both had bank accounts in our child's name and we both are contributing. Just think if we talked to each other daily, keeping each other motivated and head strong because this parenting thing isn't easy. Just think if we talked about programs to put our child in, and who is paying for what, and stayed consistent with it. Just think, if our current partners understood the task at hand, and we all had group convos about our households and ways to win. Just think if we had the resources that offered discounts and special treatment and I put you onto them as well to save you money. We can really help each other move better and more effective. We owe it to our child, but most importantly to ourselves. Let's have some real conversations and get this good life crackin'!"

Chapter 5

The Predicament We Create When We Don't Do Our Part

Now before you read this chapter, please be aware that I do go hard for a second. This is merely a vent from the accumulation of parents that have reached out to me with their frustrations. This isn't a personal moment for me, this is basically a wake up call for any parents out there that do not understand the struggles of parenting. I just wanted to put that disclaimer out there because this is real. Life is real! We have people that are walking around and not realizing the damages they are causing. So read this chapter with an open mind. If you are one of the parents that this chapter pertains to, don't get defensive. Do better! You have time!

The typical day as a parent is active to say the least. One thing for certain, parenting is a full-time job. It is a 24-hour and 365-day maintenance job. This job comes first before anything. Or does it? Unfortunately, the way our world is set up, too many of us must put our financial job before our child. How many of us have to miss out on school activities because we have to work? It happens. Let's talk about the typical day.

You wake up, wake up your child, and you get on them to get dressed for school. You might help them get ready by helping them brush their teeth & wash up. You might have ironed their clothes. You might cook breakfast. Then you are off to taking them to school, or the bus stop. You might go to work and if something happens, then you are called. You might have to take time and set up dentist appointments, vision check-ups, physicals, etc. You have to pick them up from school or after school day care. You then must listen to them talk about their day. Whether you are cooking dinner or buying dinner, sitting and eating through the meal is important. You may have to help with homework. Before you know it, now it is 8 pm and you are having your child get ready for school the next day. You might have to help with showers or getting clothes ready for the next day, you might have laundry to do, etc. Then you see them to bed. Sending your child off to bed every night with great thoughts is wise. If you read something motivational, or just having a thought-provoking conversation with them is helpful. Then it is time to relax and get things in order for you, which might leave you with a little bit of time. NOW, if you are a co-parent and you do NOT do any of these things throughout the day, you are creating a predicament for your child and your co-parent. You are a problem! You are not carrying your weight and you are creating added stress on your co-parent AND your child. As you already read, parenting is a 24-hour job EVERY DAY OF THE WEEK!! If you are a single parent and you aren't getting any help, it takes a toll on your mental and your physical being. There is no way you can provide 100% energy, drive, and stimulation to a child if you are the only one contributing. It is a huge disservice to your child and co-parent when you don't help out. Even an hour a day would be appreciated. There are people out there that know their child is being taken care of 24 hours each day, and they don't come around at all. If you are one of these parents, it would be nice to maybe drop off a meal for your child every once in a while. That would go a long way. It will give you a chance to show your child they matter. Trust me, they pay attention and notice if they are being neglected.

If you are one of the parents that are "getting off easy" - not providing any time and no effort to your child, just know you can't prosper from this. You will always subconsciously be reminded of your lack of commitment and compassion to your child. You will suffer from depression; feelings of failure, and the universe will not consistently reward you. You might feel like you are getting off easy, but that doesn't last forever. You also are missing out on the benefits of watching your child grow. Not only that, but watching your child grow and creating bonds actually help motivate your spirit. Your child brings out the best in you. So, all of these things you are missing out on, and you're most likely creating damage to your surroundings. Like I previously stated, a power couple is the best asset your child can have. If you aren't carrying your weight, you basically are putting 18 years of work onto your co-parent. Sucks! They didn't ask for the entire responsibility by themselves. Don't put your child at a disadvantage. Think of all the activities at school you can be a part of.

Think about the meals you can drop by the house a few times a week. Think about a book you can read all the way through to your child. Think about the phone calls that are needed to just listen to your son/daughter. Every little bit helps, but there is NO LIMIT on how much you can provide or do for your child. Be there! Be present! Be a factor! Otherwise, you helped create a life with someone, and you are contributing unhealthy living for your child and your co-parent. Do you understand the stress that comes along with juggling work and home alone with a child? Do you understand the stress that is created by your child crying because of your absence? Do you understand the added stress that is created by having to explain to your child that you aren't able to do it all by yourself, or the stress from having to explain where you are when you need to be standing up to the plate? Sometimes your co-parent isn't able to save as much for your child's college fund because they exhausted every financial gain to make sure your child ate. This is a cold world filled with people walking away from responsibilities that are so important. The role of a parent to some is so undervalued. Get your world together for your babies.

"The cycle needs to be broken, which is the cycle of single parenting that you are putting me through. I'm being a parent from the time I get up in the morning until the time I fall asleep, I am doing OUR job. I didn't ask for this. Who are you to have the power of making my life harder? I can walk away too. I can be just like you, no one is making me be a parent. Matter of fact, there are programs now that you would think want me to abandon our child and they would be glad to take our child away. I can get up every day like you without a care in the world. Do you know what it feels like to have to think about another human being every time you buy something to eat? Like you must think about your child and what they want to eat EVERY TIME you eat, for at least 18 years. At least help me through a little. We created life together, and our child is beautiful. Look at how much he/she looks like you. You know your child has the same traits as you do. If anyone can help handle their behavior, it would be you. Be there to help your child understand who they are. Time is everything. Money is needed but the time is crucial. Be about your people, and get fulfillment out of life."

Chapter 6
Life Twists

Boy, oh boy, life throws some curveballs, huh? Like one minute you can be up, taking trips living life and the next, you might have a family member become ill, and you might have to sell the spare car to help with hospital bills. You might walk into work one day and everyone is packing up their belongings because the company went under. Next thing you know you have a severance and 90 days to figure it all out. EVERYONE goes through ups and downs. No one is exempt! You might come home thinking life is grand and your 15-year-old daughter drops a positive pregnancy test on the table. Now you are trying to figure the next move out. This is LIFE. This is what we indirectly signed up for. I say indirectly because we didn't ask to be here. Your child is here because of your actions.

Rule # 1: Don't hide your faults and mistakes, just fight through them. Don't be humiliated about how life is going. Trust me, everyone has or will go through some humbling times. It is a part of life. I remember I filed for bankruptcy in 2005. I wanted to cut some bills out of the way and start fresh. I would tell people I just filed for bankruptcy and some would say, " Wow, you aren't embarrassed?" or " You don't think that is private?"... NO, to both questions. First, you aren't a failure. You have made some mistakes, like everyone else. If I wasn't upfront about my bankruptcy, and allowed myself to focus with my future plans, I wouldn't have been able to buy a $150,000.00 house a year later. I didn't hide my hand. I dealt with my situation and fought. However, a lot of us are scared to tell our co-parents we are down for the moment. We hide our financial crisis; we hide our mistakes because we don't want people to look down on us. We never want an ex to look at us as if they are better off without us. We must realize one thing. The only people that look down on you because of life's twists not going your way, are people that haven't gone through your situations YET! But, guaranteed they will go through something before it's all over. Don't ever be ashamed of making a mistake because as long as you recognize it and deal with it, there is nothing to feel bad about. Now, how does this play apart in your child's life? Well, first they need to see mistakes & how you play those mistakes. Secondly, you need to communicate your "downfalls" with your co-parent so they can properly manage the void that may have your child at a disadvantage. You never want your child suffering over your selfish and childish behaviors and feelings. If you have your car being repossessed, let your co-parent know it might be a second before you get another vehicle. Your co-parent can then take some steps in order to make sure their kid is good. No communication creates chaos.

Life twists happen to everyone. We must be responsible through it all. We must realize that we are all learning life as we go. The powers that be haven't always made the right education easily accessible. They don't even teach you about taxes in most High schools. Not everyone is good at managing money, dealing with emotional issues, solving problems, etc. Some of us really have a hard time in this world. There isn't a test that we all take that gives us a certification to become a parent. Regardless of your background, emotional IQ, finances, or mentality, you can become a parent. Be mindful of this when you have a child with someone. Allow them to tell you things without casting judgement. If you went to the doctor and were diagnosed with depression, feel ok with telling someone this. Feel ok with telling your co-parent this. They might be going through the same thing. They might know a natural way of dealing with it that might help you. At least they will have the knowledge of this and should be able to help out more. They might be able to take your child more and let you get the proper treatment needed.

This life is not easy. We all need help from time to time. Be the help every once in a while. Provide for your co-parent if they are taking care of your child. Providing might be giving a ride every now and then. Providing might be giving a motivational talk every now and again. Helping empowers you both.

"We both need help from time to time. As long as we keep striving and going forward, that is all that matters. Life is unpredictable. We never know what will happen. But one thing is for sure, as a parent of my child, if you are doing what you are supposed to do, I must be on your team. I must help you win, if I am able. There is no need to say I told you so, if you get in a bind. There is no need to shame you. Let's just pick up the pieces and keep it movin'. The more you are truthful with me, the better I can assist our child. Only selfish, insecure people will hide their deficits when kids are involved. If it affects my child, I need to know. If I am in a situation where I get myself into something too heavy, it is my duty to let you know. You might need to come grab our child for a little bit. Partnerships are important for this."

Chapter 7
Set Your Child Up to Win

Do you have life insurance? This is a guaranteed payment. Does your child? How about a savings account? College fund? Is your child an authorized signer on your credit cards? How many extra-curricular activities are your children involved in? Do they have access to the internet?

These are questions that need to be answered.

A lot of us graduated high school without a plan, no money and no vision. We were told to go get a job. We started working and got caught up in the rat race. Next thing you know, we were addicted to the comfort of a paycheck. Nowadays, without leaving your house, you can make money on your own. These are the days where you can honestly make six figures from your living room. The sky's the limit! There are endless possibilities, the only thing we as parents MUST do is educate ourselves. We must unlearn the old ways, and learn the new ways. This is the only way we can set our child up to win. Back when we were in school, it was different. We could really make a decent living working at a company for 20 years. Now, you can, but our kids are not built like that now. They were born into the internet. They have Google at their fingertips. They were born into convenience. The ways to make money have changed. Look at retail. Malls all over the country are shutting down and people get their clothes shipped to their doorstep. How do you set up your child to win from this? Maybe by teaching them how to sew and do alterations? Clothing is bought on the internet, but who is altering the clothes for a perfect fit? There is a future for alterations specialists. This is one example of life changing & having to deal with the world on its own terms.

Two parents coming together to raise a child and give them the tools to win are what breaks the cycle. I love when I see two parents together. Usually this means that the child has advantages. Building relationships with people and their kids help set your kids up to win. Do what you need to do to help the process.

Life insurance is important as well. You never know when it's your turn to go. We can guarantee death though. That is the only thing we can be sure about LOL. We will be gone one day, and what you leave behind can help your child.

"It's up to us to sit down and think about the future. Let's sit down and make a plan to make this life as easy as possible for our child. I am adding our child to my credit cards so when he/she reaches 28, they already have an established credit score with high numbers. We can purchase certificates of deposit with higher interest rates, so when they mature, we can keep rolling them over on our child's name. We can buy stocks and gold and silver. It would be great to be able to leave property. Let's put a plan together to make that happen. I'm not big on college nowadays, but if they want to go, let's have this money build and set aside for our child. Our child must have tons of money in order to survive. Let's give our child a head start. Nothing is more gratifying than seeing our seeds win."

Chapter 8
Child Support

I'm going to tell you right now, the child support system is so flawed, it almost makes no sense. If you can work out arrangements without child support recovery being in your business, I would definitely recommend it. There are several reasons I think child support is the worst. First, child support is not adequate compensation for parenthood. Time spent with your child is worth more, MOST of the time. If your co-parent is mentally ok, I would recommend more time spent than dealing with money instead.

Another reason is the calculations for child support vary so much, and it is so hard to determine what is a fair amount to give. There is no way to track exactly how much of it is actually going towards your child. The argument from some receivers is that you shouldn't worry about where the money is spent, and I agree to a certain extent. Maybe your child support check is reimbursement for the month. Maybe the whole check goes towards rent. Your child lives there, so that makes sense.

The other big issue is the person getting hit for child support is most likely not making enough to survive. That parent probably works two to three jobs trying to make ends meet. This does drain the energy of that parent, and they may not have the energy for any time spent. They may not have the time. Also, as we discussed before how life happens, if there are circumstances that prevent you from working, this creates difficulties with the co-parent. Don't get me wrong, sometimes a third party is a necessity to provide structure, but if you can work it out between the two of you, it can work. This makes for less stress, less paperwork and more flexibility. Everyone involved needs to be accountable, definitely! We need both parents to take care of responsibility, but sometimes, child support creates division and hostility. If the child support isn't on agreeable terms, then problems between the two of you will arise.

Some people don't want to go through the hassle of putting the co-parent on child support. This is totally a judgement call. Some parents will quit their jobs if they feel there is a threat of child support. This may cause the parent to not be able to help at all financially. I encourage everyone to have a real conversation with their co-parent. I encourage all co-parents to develop a child support system that works for them and everyone involved. It is needed, you should be helping financially with your child.

"Let's be real, do we want these people in our business? Let's have less paperwork and let's help each other make the best out of this. Let's sit down with each other and really go over expenses. You might not want to pay a lot and I get it. Maybe we can work out other ways to compensate. Maybe instead of money, just take care of all the school clothes and come get your child every other weekend. Maybe money isn't the best answer. Maybe you can pick up the child every day and feed him/her dinner. It takes us sitting down & working out a routine that works for us. Let's dig deeper than just

49

"$300 a month". Let's think of our daily lives and what our biggest challenges are, and then go from there. You might not be a morning person so instead of money, maybe you would rather me come pick up our child every morning and drop them off to school? That would work out for me because your house is on the way to my job in the morning. This works out great for us. There are tons of ways we can help each other besides just a monthly check. Let's be adults and work this out. Showing that our child is much more than some cash would be more beneficial."

Outro: I want us all to win. I love seeing families together, sticking through the tough times and helping each other through the struggle. I see how important it is to really be a factor in your child's life. It is tough going through the motions with someone if you do not understand them. Here is what I truly recommend that you do with your co-parent. These are in no particular order.

Take a weekend (if you can) away from the world and really have some conversations.

Discuss this book and any other conversations you need to get off of your chest. During this weekend, have your child present for a lot of it. Have your current significant others there for a lot of it. Family is everything. During this weekend, have some team building exercises. Like seriously, this might sound corny, however, million-dollar companies exercise these games to build engagement and a sense of togetherness. This is what we need. Get out of your own feelings & immaturities and grow bonds with each other. For the parent "couples" that don't have significant others, do these things with just your co-parent and your child, or invite grandparents, or other family members.

Do these retreats quite frequently. Stay consistent.

Hold each other accountable. How? Sit down with your co-parent and go over your goals, dreams, and visions. Go over what you think is best for your child. I'm sure a lot of passionate conversations from the heart will come about if you both will set your ego and immaturity aside, and really use time to build thoughts around your child. When you put your visions and goals in the ears of other people, those people can hold you accountable. If you are doing something that doesn't align with your dreams and visions, you have a "teammate" letting you know you are off track. We all need that from time to time.

Stand up! No really. You made your situation, now make it the best! Understand you have the biggest part in making it a blessing. You are the piece that can make this work. Take your time and think through with logic.

Taking time to really get to know each other deeper will make it easier to communicate. We must learn how to understand each other's point of view. We should ask more questions. We should know about each other's childhoods and develop an understanding of why we think the way we do. Everyone speaks a different language. The language we speak is from years of conditioned thoughts that have molded us. We must respect that. I used to yell all the time to try and get my point across. One reason was because when I was younger, I used to hang out with older people, and my voice would get drowned out by their bigger and more boisterous voices. I would always get cut off like what I had to say didn't matter. This is an example of what your co-parent might have an issue with.

DON'T TAKE IT PERSONAL!!! How many times have you been in a situation with someone for the first time, and they are scared? Like going on a roller coaster ride and the people behind you are screaming in your ear. Did you take it personal? No! They had to let out a scream because that was the best way they knew how to deal with the situation of being in the air being jerked every which way with no control. Relate the feelings of riding on the roller coaster to that of finding out you were having this baby with all of those emotions, right? Allow each other to have different coping mechanisms. Talk about them. Motivate each other to get past them. Feel each other's energy. Write each other notes as much as possible. It doesn't matter if you wanted this or not, you are here. Help each other be the best you can be. Helping each other helps your legacy, your family, and your family name. Helping each other helps life. It helps shape our futures. Be a power couple and raise these babies to a high standard!

Bonus

It's Not About You (a message from your child)

As I open my eyes and see the world for the first time, I want to thank you for my life. I don't know what to expect, but this seems like the place to be. It seems like there are so many opportunities here. It seems like I can grow and be who I want to be. This seems like you wanted me here, so I am here. Now why the hell are you not taking care of me?? I didn't ask for this! I didn't ask to be here, YOU created me! I am the innocent one here. As I grow, I see how hard this world can be. Why aren't you here teaching me? You know more than I do. Well, I had my first choir concert today. I understand you couldn't come because you were working, but you couldn't call and ask me how it went? Well, just so you know I was nervous. I got in my first fight the other day as well. You would have been proud. I was losing at first, but I came back and won. I'm getting it, I'm learning how to be tough. Don't you worry, my heart is adapting to this cold world. How about stop arguing so much with the partner you created me with. You both have a job to do. Why are you not figuring out how to make my life easier?

I'm in high school now. I saw you drive past me the other day. You didn't even stop. I bet you were busy. I'm busy too. I'm busy trying to figure out how to finish this school thing. I don't want to go, honestly. I hate it. Anyway, everyone says I look just like you. I wouldn't know as I hardly see you. Maybe we will catch up one day and talk about my pains from you not being there. My pains from you arguing all the time on the phone with my "real" parent. Since you brought me into this cold world, do you have a business I can run so I don't have to slave for someone else? Can you teach me a trade? Teach me about love and respect. Also, why do you talk about my other parent so bad? Do you not know I am them? You don't think that hurts me? You laid down and had me. Was I a mistake? You didn't really want me? Anyway, it's not about you anymore. It's not about your feelings, or your wants. Hello! It's me! I'm here now. Grow up and take care of me. Guide me, teach me! You brought me in this world and now I'm just wondering aimlessly listening to people tell me what to do, and they don't care about me. Well, anyway I gotta go. I'm stressed. My parent, your co-parent is yelling at me saying I'm acting just like you, and I need to go and figure out my place in this world that I didn't ask to be in. Thanks for letting me rant, but it's getting harder and I guess this is my cry for help. Get it together and help me win.

Peace and love until next time. Follow me on social media at drmartinsr on instagram and John Martin Sr. on Facebook. Visit www.8conversationstohave.com to stay in tune with future and past publications.